Color Pictures

March 3 – April 14, 2012
Organized by Frances Colpitt

John Baldessari · Sarah Charlesworth · William Eggleston · Russell Lee · Thomas Ruff · Stephen Shore · Allison V. Smith · Ann Stautberg

Fort Worth Contemporary Arts

2900 W. Berry Street Fort Worth TX 76109

theartgalleries.tcu.edu theartgalleries@tcu.edu

Color Pictures
Published by The Art Galleries at TCU

Color Pictures
3 March – 14 April 2012
Fort Worth Contemporary Arts

The Art Galleries at TCU
Texas Christian University
2800 South University Drive
Fort Worth, Texas 76129 USA
817.257.2588
www.theartgalleries.tcu.edu theartgalleries@tcu.edu

Essays © Melissa Barry, David Cavaliero, Frances Colpitt, Devon Nowlin, Christina Rees, Gregory Ruppe, Meg Smith, Zoetina Veal.

Exhibition Curator: Frances Colpitt
Curator of the Art Galleries at TCU: Christina Rees
Editors: David Cavaliero, Devon Nowlin, Meg Smith
Designer: Allie Regan Dickerson
Installation Photography: Bradly Brown

The Art Galleries at TCU
PRINTED IN AN EDITION OF 500, MARCH 2012.

Color Pictures: 3 March - 14 April 2012, Fort Worth Contemporary Arts.
ISBN 978-0-9801617-2-4

Cover: Sarah Charlesworth, *Relative Values, Maximum Hues,* 2006

Printed in Fort Worth

In Loving Memory of Kodak

Lenders to the Exhibition

Michael Auping, Fort Worth, TX

Barry Whistler Gallery, Dallas, TX

Margo Leavin Gallery, Los Angeles, CA

Catherine and Will Rose, Dallas, TX

The Rachofsky Collection, Dallas, TX

Table of Contents

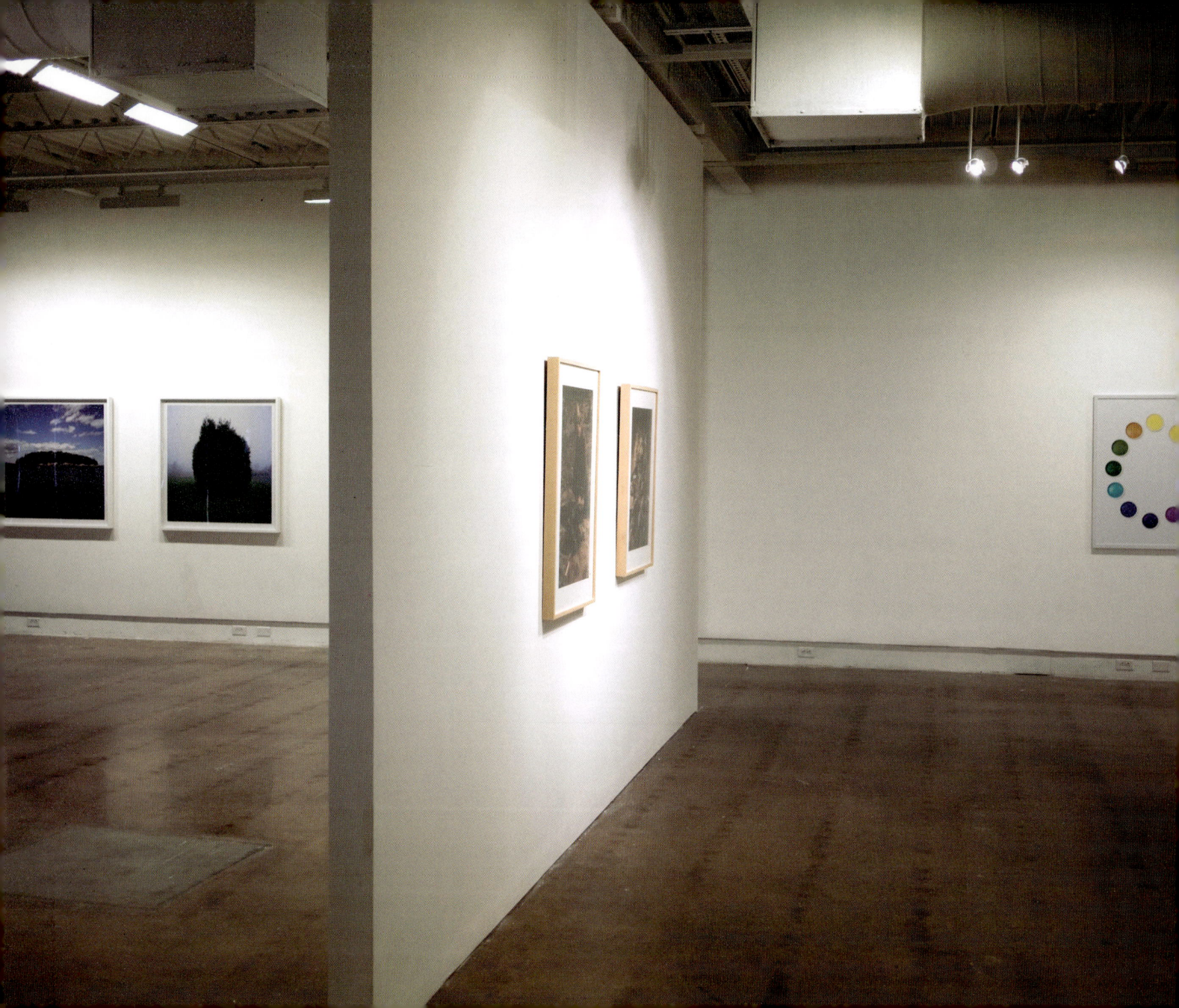

Introduction

Frances Colpitt

"Color Pictures" arose from my graduate art history seminar on photography last spring, Photography In/As/Not as Art (a title unintentionally pilfered from Jeff Wall's 1995 landmark essay, "'Marks of Indifference': Aspects of Photography in, or as, Conceptual Art"). When the Fort Worth Contemporary Arts (FWCA) programming committee identified the need for a photography exhibition, I volunteered the subject of the class, which explored the nexus of visual art and photography in the 1970s. During the decade, conceptual artists made liberal use of photographs to record their ideas while the work of photographers appeared to "ascend" to the long-awaited status of fine art. Irrespective of recent photographic technology, color seemed to be a common *subject matter* for artists and contemporary photographers and therefore a fitting theme for this exhibition. The catalogue essayists and seminar participants—three of whom are finished with their studies and pursuing their careers—have been a constant source of inspiration, advice, and knowledge, and the true professionals we at TCU consider them to be throughout their graduate training.

As an artistic medium, photography developed a distinct aesthetic and technical path. From Alfred Stieglitz to Ansel Adams, photography was conceived as a means for personal and subjective expression or, in the hands of Paul Strand and Lazlo Moholy-Nagy, creative experiment, culminating in the late-twentieth-century designation "art-photography." This term has the benefit of distinguishing the *auteur* (following the French veneration of their film directors) from the amateur or hobbyist photographer, as well as from the documentarian and photojournalist. In the 1960s, however, many former painters adopted the camera to advance the reductive, anti-aesthetic tendency of late modernism, jettisoning their paint and canvases along with the long-forsaken rationale of beauty. The "dematerialization of art" shifted the emphasis from the photograph as an art object to the photograph as a mere document, more important for what it says about the world than about the artist. In a groundbreaking exhibition of 1978, mingling the photographs and photographic prints of artists and art-photographers, curator John Szarkowski divided the show's participants into "those who think of [photography] as a means of self-expression and those who think of it as a method of exploration."[1]

Concurrent with the widespread use of the camera by artists, art-photography began to migrate from its isolation in specialized galleries, private collections, and publications, which were usually different from those populated by painting and sculpture. It looked as if photography was finally prevailing in Stieglitz's campaign, beginning in the late nineteenth century, for the recognition of the medium as a legitimate form of art, equal to painting in every way. This transition, however, was not smooth or uncontested. Many magazine and exhibition catalogue essays examined and continue to unpack the crossover, noting, at first, how very different the approaches of photographers and artists were and, finally, how fully photography has been absorbed by the art world. While late modernist photography strove for formal and medium-specific achievements, wrote critic Nancy Foote in 1976, "conceptual art exhibits little photographic self-consciousness, setting itself apart from so-called serious photography by a snapshot-like amateurism and nonchalance that would raise the hackles of any earnest professional."[2] With precedence in the readymades of Marcel Duchamp, in which handicraft is exchanged for intellect, this attitude is consistent with the phenomenon of "deskilling" in modern art.[3] There are parallels, of course, between *choosing* a readymade and *taking* a photograph. Eschewing formally compelling composition and subjective content, the photographs of John Baldessari and Ed Ruscha are deliberately un-artistic; "photography degree zero," Lewis Baltz called it, when first confronted with Ruscha's books of photographs.[4]

The first major exhibition to acknowledge the influence of conceptualism on photography was "New Topographics: Photographs of a Man-Altered Landscape" at the George Eastman House in Rochester, New York, in 1975. The show brought together the work of 11 photographers, including the team of Bernd and Hilla Becher, Baltz, and Stephen Shore, to argue for a new anti-picturesque that was seemingly objective and without "style" in the depiction of the rural, industrial, and suburban landscape. While Ruscha was perhaps the central figure in this development, his work was not included since curator William Jenkins believed that its concerns were artistic rather than photographic, an exclusion he later regretted.[5] With a background in commercial art and painting, Ruscha turned to photography to make concept-driven but finely made books produced in small editions. The idea for the title of his first book, *Twentysix Gasoline Stations* (1963), came before the pictures themselves, which were accordingly compiled to fill in the pages. As a young artist, he frequently drove 1,400 miles from his home in Los Angeles to Oklahoma City, where his family lived, and remarked that "there was so much wasteland between L.A. and Oklahoma that somebody had to bring the news to the city."[6] The fulfillment of Ruscha's conceptual project is reminiscent of Russell Lee's documentary photographs for the Farm Security Administration (FSA) during the Depression. Traveling primarily to small towns in the West, Lee produced thousands of black-and-white negatives and color transparencies for the FSA. Like Ruscha, his photographs are serial, in a straightforward style of reportage, which led FSA director, Roy Stryker, to describe him as a "taxonomist with a camera;" Dorothea Lange called him "the great cataloguer." Sol LeWitt's characterization of the conceptual artist as a "clerk cataloguing the results of his premise" is as applicable to Lee as to Ruscha.[7]

Following a few experiments such as Duchamp's and Man Ray's photographic collaborations in the 1920s and Warhol's adaption of photo-silkscreen in 1962, conceptual artists introduced photography into their work between 1966 and 1968. Usually accompanied by explanatory texts, the use of photographs facilitated artistic communication, bypassing the reproductive stage in catalogues and periodicals that withhold such pertinent information as actual size and color, texture and dimension, brushwork or patina, and especially what Walter Benjamin defined as the "aura" of the original. The reproduction of a photo or text functions as "primary information," according to Seth Siegelaub, communicating to the viewer/reader the same content it conveys hanging on the gallery wall.[8] The form of these early photographic projects often resembled snapshots (a comparison also leveled at seemingly uncomposed images by art-photographers such as William Eggleston). Excepting Dan Graham and his early photo-essay *Homes for America* (1966), John Baldessari and Douglas Huebler were the first to consistently include photographs in their work. Unlike many later conceptualists who were amateur photographers or relied on professionals to document their projects, Baldessari and Huebler were familiar and experienced with the medium. Attributing the "beauty" of his work to its systematic structure, Huebler also admitted that he "created 'well-made' images, 'in the sense that they were technically perfect.'"[9] Although Baldessari is not known for his technical skills (preferring the efficiency of commercial labs), he began processing his own photographs in high school, even winning a national scholastic competition with them. A painter since the early 1950s, Baldessari's first incorporation of photography in his paintings is legendary: dissatisfied with relational composition, or part-to-part balance, and the absurdity of putting one color next to another, as well as "to give people what they want" and understand by using language and photographs, he adopted the photo-silkscreen process to transfer his black-and-white snapshots to canvas and used a sign painter to letter them with art-related texts. Like most artists in the '60s, he was intent on avoiding aesthetic decisions and expressive, personal style, reducing his process to one of "choosing."[10]

Although they often used less expensive black-and-white

film, conceptualists had no prohibition or prejudice against color photography; Baldessari, for example, has used it consistently since 1969. In art-photography color was nearly forbidden. One reason for this was practical, given the development of technology and its correlated expense. Although experimental color processes were theoretically available to professionals in the early twentieth century, the complexities of processing and the questionable quality of printing were prohibitive. The dye-transfer process made color more available (though still expensive and time consuming), thus it was more widely used in industry, especially in magazine advertising. Color, as Naomi Rosenblum pointed out, glamorized its subject and seduced its consumers, particularly during the frugal years of the 1930s. The sober poverty of the Depression, however, might have appeared less evocative in color, which left publishers disinclined to print the few hundred color photographs commissioned by the FSA between 1935 and 1943.[11] Color technology, particularly Kodak's, was instrumental, as well. Kodacolor, color negative film that facilitated color prints, was not available until 1942. Kodachrome, motion picture positive film and sheet positive film (for slides and transparencies) that required return to Kodak for processing, was introduced in the mid-1930s. It defined amateur slide-photography, surging in the '50s and '60s, to the point that Stephen Shore's radical

color work could evoke, among other things, a "Kodachrome amateur outlook" according to curator Michael Auping.[12] Kodak—filing for bankruptcy just this year—was so definitive of photographic art, industry, and commerce that Jean-Luc Godard dismissed his own auteurism in the 1960s, saying "Kodak does 98 percent."[13] On a scale comparable to color, the development of digital imagery and Photoshop, released in 1990, transformed photography (and, fatally, Kodak), altering the "indexical" relationship of the photograph to observable reality.[14] "Since the photographic medium has been digitized," Andreas Gursky observed, "a fixed definition of the term 'photography' has become impossible."[15] A similar skepticism informs Thomas Ruff's digital photographs of Mies van der Rohe's German Pavilion, a recently reconstructed building only known by recent generations through black-and-white photographs. Ruff's alteration of the color of the Pavilion's curtain explores the gap between seeing and knowing.

As common—though by no means omnipresent—as the color art photograph is today, its acceptance was hard won. Many critics interpreted color as too commercial, given its pervasive use in magazine advertising and Hollywood film in the mid-century years. Worse, its effects were condemned as unrealistic, in part due to early color's intensely saturated hues, and as garish or "vulgar," in Walker Evans's opinion.

As the technology improved, so did photography's realism: its resemblance to the actual appearance of things. A revised critique as *too* realistic underlay the hostile responses to Eggleston's 1976 exhibition of color photographs at the Museum of Modern Art in New York, the first granted by the institution to the medium. According to his critics, his humble subjects such as a tricycle or a pair of shoes failed to transcend their pedestrian origins, in contrast to, for example, Edward Weston's elegant bell pepper or seashell in black and white. Coloristically, as well as compositionally, Eggleston's work was derided by conservative critic Hilton Kramer as "snapshot chic."[16] The persistence of Eggleston and Shore (and, arguably, the example of Paul Outerbridge in the 1930s) redefined photography to the same extent as advancements in technology and the influence of conceptualism on "New Topographics."

Finally, the acceptance of color photographs was facilitated by the same reason it remained forbidden for so long: its pervasiveness in commercial media, including color magazine ads, photojournalism, and the movies. At the pinnacle of the television age in 1965, more than half of the programming was in color and, before the end of the '70s, more than three-fourths of American homes had color TV sets. Photography's insistence on black and white denied this common reality.

Coinciding with the rise of color was the acceptance of photography by the art world, in which women played a transformative role. Launching their careers in the late 1970s, many of the most prominent artists of the '80s were not only women but photographers. The choice of the photographic medium was an intentional refusal of *painting*, modernism's preeminent—and definitively masculine—art form. Abandoning the phallic paintbrush, they also rejected painting's "signs of artistic labor—violent, 'impassioned' brushwork, for example . . . simulacra of mastery . . . virility, masculinity, [and] potency." Furthermore, Craig Owens maintained, the anti-patriarchic technique of photographic appropriation in the work of Sherrie Levine, and more generally, Barbara Kruger, Cindy Sherman, Louise Lawler, and Sarah Charlesworth, represents "a refusal of the role of creator as 'father' of the work."[17] While many women artists began their careers working in less expensive black and white, like many photographers, they moved into color in the '80s. Color's feminizing effect, long acknowledged in painting and sculpture,[18] partially contributed to its new status in photography. Simultaneously, women, color, and photography began to fully participate in the art world.

The development of Charlesworth's work, in particular, reflects the changing role of photography in contemporary art-making. From her early black-and-white appropriations of newspaper pages to her recent semi-abstract color compositions, her work progressed from the anti-aesthetic of conceptual art to the evocative visuality of photographic art. Current wisdom maintains that there is no longer any qualitative distinction between art made with a paintbrush and that made with a camera. The blurring of the boundaries between artistic mediums—dolefully predicted by Michael Fried in 1967 and analyzed by Rosalind Krauss as the "post-medium condition"—resulted in "generic art," according to Thierry de Duve, without a definitive foundation in any particular material or technique.[19] But such democratic optimism isn't completely borne out by the mechanics of the art world. Recently hailed by the New York Times for "taking photography out of a ghetto and putting it on the same firm fine-art footing as painting and sculpture," Sherman is not universally appreciated as merely a *photographer*. In a lengthy footnote, Fried argued that she is "interesting as an artist but uninteresting as a photographer," in Peter Bunnell's words.[20] Many in the photography community still consider themselves distinct from the art community, particularly with respect to the market. The rarity and fragility of historical photographs, their fugitive tones and colors, have made them potentially more precious than many paintings. Despite Benjamin's definition of photography as inherently multiple—"to ask for the 'authentic' print makes no sense"—its status as a collectible counters philosophical arguments. One could, of course, argue the same for conceptual photographs, intended as documents, worthless objects in themselves, which time has transformed into valuable artifacts.

Market forces aside, the differences between art (or painting, the modernist model of art) and photography have for all purposes collapsed in postmodernism. "We must no longer speak of photography as art, but of art as photography," Jean Clair wrote in 1973, and "consider the medium as a tool for artistic expression rather than make it into an 'art in and unto itself,'" added Jean-François Chevrier.[21] Photography remains different from painting, but painting itself is different from (modernist) painting, to the extent that it has opened itself to extra-painting issues. Painting and photography have been absorbed by (post-medium) art, where both are used as art-making procedures. As Fried and Chevrier acknowledged, recent photography's large scale and frontality have replaced the earlier tradition of photographs—whether conceptual, like Baldessari's, or artistic, like Eggleston's and Shore's—destined for the hand-held book, magazine, or storage box. The new photographs—such as Charlesworth's and Allison V. Smith's—are made for the wall, pictures like any others.

Notes

1. John Szarkowski, *Mirrors and Windows: American Photography since 1960* (New York: The Museum of Modern Art, 1978), 11.

2. Nancy Foote, "The Anti-Photographers," in T*he Last Picture Show: Artists Using Photography 1960-1982*, ed. Douglas Fogle (Minneapolis: Walker Art Center, 2003), 24. See Wall's essay in the same volume.

3. John Roberts, "Art After Deskilling," *Historical Materialism* 18 (2010): 83-86.

4. Britt Salvesen, ed., "New Topographics," in *New Topographics* (Göttingen, Germany: Steidl, 2009), 26. This essay accompanied a reprise of the exhibition in Los Angeles in 2010.

5. Ibid, 27.

6. Patricia Failing, "Ruscha, Young Artist," in *Leave Any Information at the Signal: Writings, Interviews, Bits, Pages*, ed. Alexandra Schwartz (Cambridge: MIT Press, 2002), 232-33.

7. Benjamin H. D. Buchloh, "From the Aesthetic of Administration to Institutional Critique," in *L'Art Conceptual, Une Perspective*, ed. Suzanne Pagé (Paris: Musée de l'Art Moderne de la Ville de Paris, 1989), 52 n. 30.

8. Charles Harrison and Seth Siegelaub, "On Exhibitions and the World at Large," in *Conceptual Art: A Critical Anthology*, ed. Alexander Alberro and Blake Stimson (Cambridge: MIT Press, 1999), 199 n. 30. Siegelaub was the foremost dealer and promoter of conceptual art, using the publishing industry to disseminate his artists' photo/text works.

9. Jean-François Chevrier, "The Adventures of the Picture Form in the History of Photography," in *The Last Picture Show*, 120.

10. See Christopher Knight, Oral history interview with John Baldessari, 1992 Apr. 4-5, Archives of American Art, Smithsonian Institution and Jeanne Siegel, "John Baldessari: Recalling Ideas," in *Art Talk: The Early 80s* (New York: Da Capo Press, 1988), 38-50.

11. Naomi Rosenblum, *A World History of Photography* (New York: Abbeville, 2007), 602-12.

12. Michael Auping, "Stephen Shore: American Photographer," *30 Years: Interviews and Outtakes* (Fort Worth: Modern Art Museum of Fort Worth, 2007), 267.

13. Quoted in Wall, "'Marks of Indifference': Aspects of Photography in, or as, Conceptual Art," in *The Last Picture Show*, 42.

14. See Rosalind E. Krauss, "Notes on the Index: Part 1," in *The Originality of the Avant-Garde and Other Modernist Myths* (Cambridge: MIT Press, 1983).

15. Quoted in Michael Fried, *Why Photography Matters as Art as Never Before* (New Haven: Yale University Press, 2008), 166.

16. Hilton Kramer, "Focus on Photo Shows," *New York Times*, May 28, 1976.

17. Craig Owens, *Beyond Recognition: Representation, Power, and Culture* (Berkeley and Los Angeles: University of California Press, 1992), 177-82.

18. See Jacqueline Lichtenstein, *The Eloquence of Color: Rhetoric and Painting in the French Classical Age*, trans. Emily McVarish (Berkeley and Los Angeles: University of California Press, 1993).

19. Michael Fried, "Art and Objecthood," in *Art and Objecthood: Essays and Reviews* (Chicago: University of Chicago Press, 1998); Rosalind Krauss, "The Post-Medium Condition" in *Perpetual Inventory* (Cambridge: MIT Press, 2010); and Thierry de Duve, "The Monochrome and the Blank Canvas," in *Kant After Duchamp* (Cambridge: MIT Press, 1999).

20. Carol Vogel, "Cindy Sherman Unmasked," *New York Times*, February 17, 2012; Fried, *Why Photography Matters*, 353-54 n. 7.

21. Chevrier, "The Adventures of the Picture Form," 113.

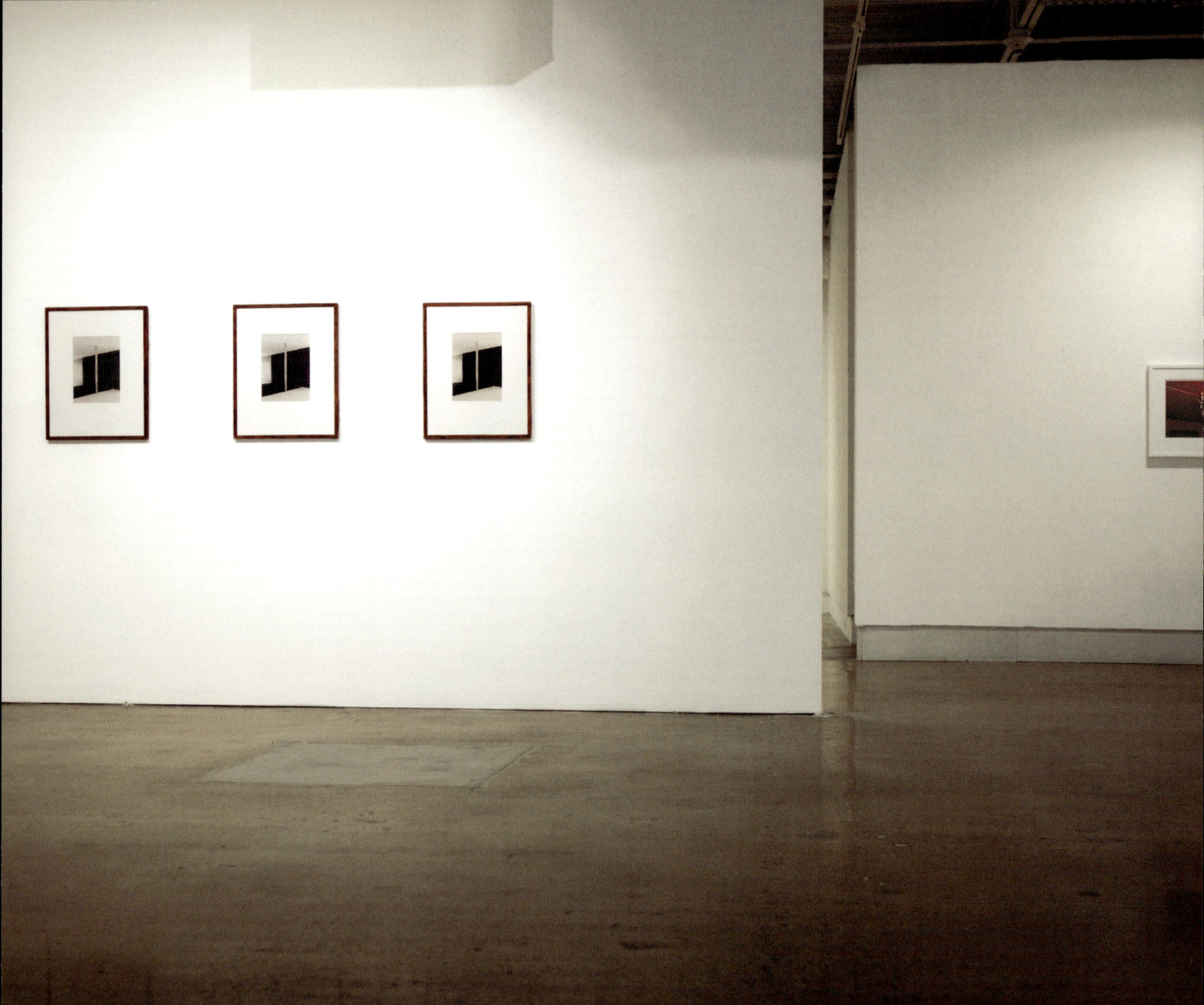

Color Pictures

John Baldessari · Sarah Charlesworth · William Eggleston · Russell Lee · Thomas Ruff · Stephen Shore · Allison V. Smith · Ann Stautberg

John Baldessari
by Christina Rees

John Baldessari (b. 1931), along with his peer Bruce Nauman, has become a leading figure of a special breed of American conceptual artist—the kind who discovers the sublime in the absurd—using the transformation of the language and meaning of photography and appropriated imagery as his primary (though not only) tool. Hailing from San Diego, Baldessari has insisted on the importance of the investigative over the explicit in art. Teaching at the California Institute of the Arts and UCLA from 1970 to 2008, he was an international influence on recent generations of artists and nearly single-handedly advanced the region's academic profile. Along with Ed Ruscha, Chris Burden, and Paul McCarthy, he effectively transformed the viability of the Los Angeles art scene. His association with the West Coast's ascension in the contemporary art world is inarguable.

There is an unapologetic and intellectual power behind his works that can startle, amuse, or intimidate the viewer, especially considering how effectively he uses such simple and unexpected sources to reach for and achieve The Idea, the lynchpin of effective conceptualism.

Baldesarri's work with color photography started early in his career, on a road trip in 1963, in which he photographed the backside of every truck he encountered on the California highway. He continued his exploration of abstracting cars' shapes and colors in his ongoing Color Car Series. In this exhibition's diptych, he plays with the notion of landscape, skyscape, and the picture plane by presenting a photographic close up of an old blue car door—dirty one day and then polished another—effectively entertaining viewers' original assumptions about what they think they know about the image on first encounter, and re-adjusting it into something factual, humorous, and prosaic.

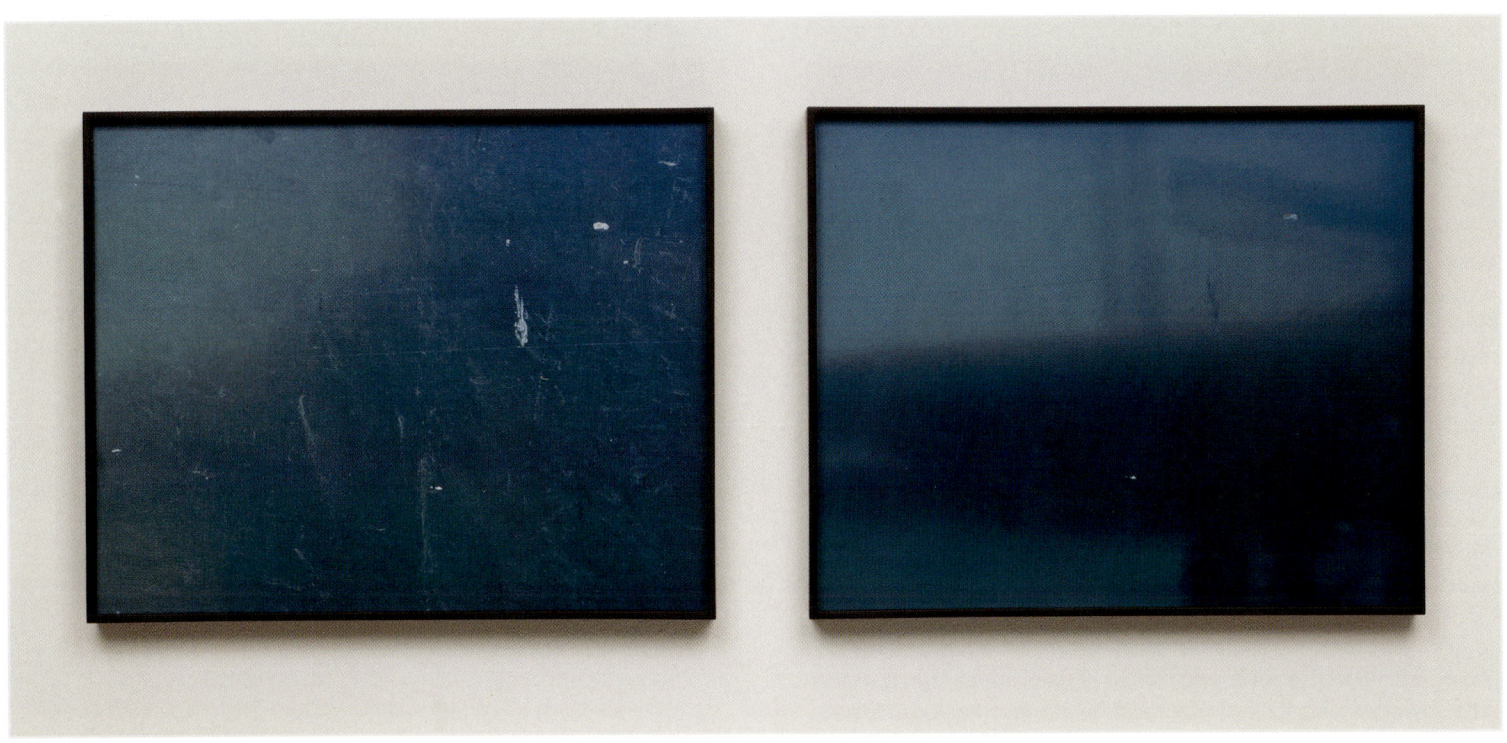

John Baldessari

Color Car Series: 1968 Volvo, Dirty and Polished, 1976/2011
Two Archival Inkjet prints, 15.75 x 19.75"; 16.25 x 20.25"

Photography by Brian Forrest

Sarah Charlesworth
by Zoetina Veal

Photography matters as art as never before because it has become the medium that raises the question of its own status as art most acutely.

—Michael Fried

The choices made by the artist Sarah Charlesworth are numerous and philosophically varied despite the first-glance simplicity and minimalist precision of her photographs.

Charlesworth's choices are layered like a wedding cake:
Photograph in **color**,
Photograph in color **of color**,
Photograph in color of **watercolor paint**,
Photograph in color of a watercolor paint **color chart**.

The visual effect is ostensibly charming, but alas, deceptive. Like a magician's sleight of hand, Charlesworth's use of the subjective psychological allure of the color spectrum distracts the viewer. Buried beneath the color is an astute discourse about intentionality, facticity, and painting in the context of photo-conceptualism.

The dishes of paint in Charlesworth's 2006 Concrete Color series were mixed precisely, set out in geometric arrangements, photographed from above, and printed in an oversize format.[1] The artist's systematic and literal approach to the work begins to break down upon a closer examination. In one of the photographs, *Small Oval*, there is a subtle deviation from the classic color chart—the pots located at the 11 o'clock and 8 o'clock positions on the wheel don't fit the pattern. In conjunction with the meticulous composition, this "tell" prevents the photograph from falling into non-art objecthood or, put another way, from being mere photographic documentation of familiar objects. Calling attention to the hidden artifice of photography as a medium by which objective reality can be conveyed, Charlesworth's ironic presentation of classic color theory charts could be considered matter-of-fact or deadpan documentation.

Charlesworth's scientific investigation of color photography is akin to the self-critical investigations of modernist painting analyzed by Clement Greenberg.[2] Mixing colors, determining their placement in relation to one another, and photographing them in an attempt to reproduce "true" hues heightens the level of artistic investigation into representation that is at once objective and abstract.[3]

1. Hilary Stunda, "Sarah Charlesworth: Baldwin," *ARTnews* 107, no. 3 (March 2008): 146.
2. Clement Greenberg, "Modernist Painting," *Art and Literature* 4 (Spring 1965): 193-201.
3. Stunda, "Sarah Charlesworth," 146.

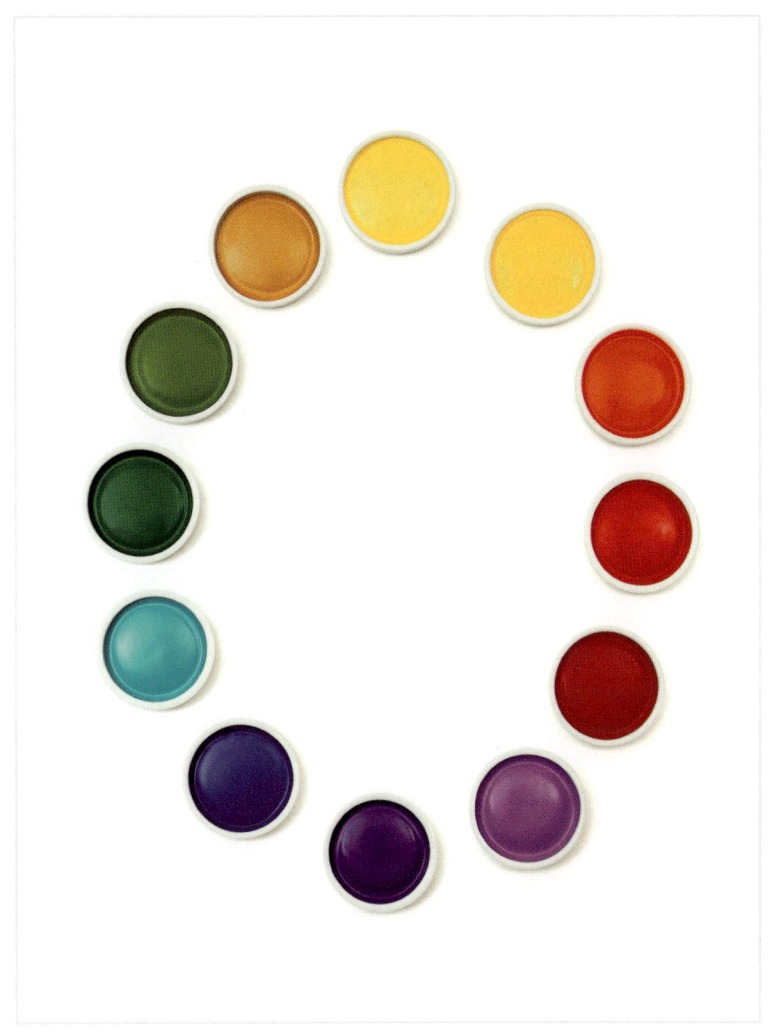

Sarah Charlesworth
Small Oval, 2006
Fuji Crystal Archive Print, 41 x 31"

William Eggleston
by David Cavaliero

The journalist, the pornographer, the esthete and the amateur enter the temple of art as equals....

—Hilton Kramer

New York Times art critic Hilton Kramer's remark, while meant as a slight toward what he termed the "snapshot chic" aesthetic of photographic work such as William Eggleston's, serves as an apt description of the complex vantage point the Memphis-based artist forces upon the viewer.[1]

Eggleston's 1976 show at the Museum of Modern Art, the institution's first major exhibition dedicated to color photographs, was panned by critics who tended to agree less with curator John Szarkowski's argument that the artist's photographs were "perfect… surrogates for the experience they pretend to record … described here with clarity, fullness, and elegance" and more with Kramer's characterization that they were "perfectly banal, perhaps. Perfectly boring, certainly…, a commonplace world of little visual interest."[2]

What Kramer and other critics failed to recognize is a question of seeing photography beyond the aesthetic trappings,standards imposed on it by a generation of practitioners who are generally considered to be the artistic progeny of photographer and art dealer Alfred Stieglitz. The discrepancy with color photography, clear in work such as Eggleston's *Greenwood, Mississippi*, (1973), is that the anti-aesthetic quality produced here is a closer representation of how the viewer sees things in real life. Edging ever closer to that boundary highlights the separation between reality and its artifice.

Because photography leads to the production of pictures, as viewers we want to impose narrative structures onto them. But those constructions are our own, and implicit in our acceptance of photography as art is an understanding that the photograph is "only a picture, a concrete kind of fiction, not to be admitted as hard evidence."[3] The photograph is an image of the photographer's choosing, in the same manner a painter or a sculptor fashions visual imagery where there once was none.

Eggleston deftly makes it seem as if his images represent reality, or at least our presumptions about it. But his work, like the way we remember things, isn't an aestheticized reality in the way a black-and-white Stieglitz photograph is; rather, it recalls images culled from memories and frugally and subjectively presents information to the viewer. It's the way our memories of color and form operate. For example, standing in a red room, one remembers a sexual poster on the wall and a single light bulb and ceiling fan. As in *Greenwood, Mississippi*, we tend to view things centered and in front of us (imagine having a face-to-face conversation, or even the act of looking at a photograph), and remember them the same way.

What makes Eggleston's images continually compelling (the artist had a retrospective at the Whitney Museum of American Art in 2008) is how he evokes this romantic association with memory. Eggleston negotiates this divide between the romanticized and the real by creating pictures that inhabit an uncomfortable domain, one that has all the detachment of a public business transaction, yet the affection of a private moment of intimacy.

1. Hilton Kramer, "The Paradoxical Museumization of Photography," *New York Times*, November 17, 1977.
2. John Szarkowski, *William Eggleston's Guide*, 2nd ed. (New York: The Museum of Modern Art, 2002), 14; and Hilton Kramer, "Focus on Photo Shows," *New York Times*, May 28, 1976.
3. Szarkowski, *William Eggleston's Guide*,14.

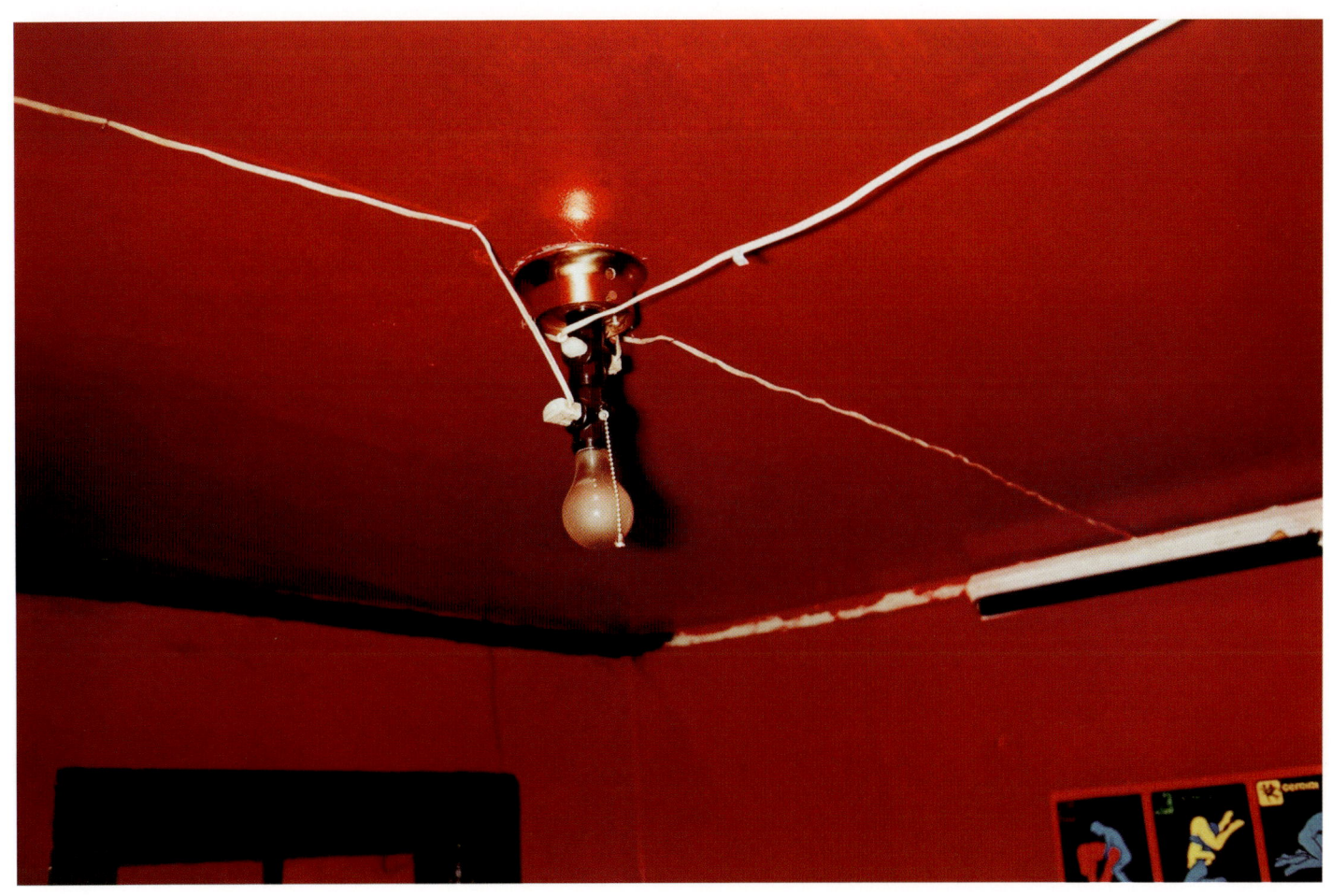

William Eggleston

Greenwood, Mississippi, 1973
Vintage dye transfer print mounted to board, 12.5 x 19"

Russell Lee
by Devon Nowlin

Thanks to the widely distributed photographic images commissioned by government agencies like the Works Progress Administration (WPA), the Farm Security Administration (FSA), and the Office of War Information (OWI), our collective visual memory of the 1930s and '40s is largely in black and white. The documentary photographs paid for with federal tax dollars are now free and made available to the public through the U.S. Library of Congress American Memory Collection. Initially compiled for historical record, this collection of black-and-white photography is now regarded as art; FSA photos by Walker Evans and Dorothea Lange are well-known examples. Especially for documentarians in the field, black-and-white film of the era was easier to handle and more affordably developed than the then-new Kodachrome or Kodacolor. Scenes in black and white also supported the goals of government agencies by heightening the subtext of despair during the Depression in order to promote New Deal policies. In this exhibition, two photographs by FSA photographer Russell Lee show how photographers used color film and transparencies to shed new light on the lives and economic times of people in the impoverished Southwest.

Before picking up his first camera at the age of 32, Russell Lee was trained as a chemical engineer and as a painter, living and working in San Francisco and Woodstock, New York. After his work for the FSA, Lee was the first Professor of Photography at the University of Texas from 1965 to 1973. Lee regarded his role in the FSA as one of a craftsman, folklorist, and taxonomist. As one of the few photographers of the time using Kodachrome, his large collection of color transparencies exemplifies the social gatherings of distinctive regional cultures, and includes images of the hard-working people whose determination lifted us out of the Depression.[1]

In *Exhibit of crops and vegetables at the Pie Town, New Mexico, Fair*, Lee presents a seemingly objective view of award-winning produce from a small town of sharecroppers and merchants in a region where his best-known photographs were taken. The scene is an example of the positive results of the community's economic circumstances: corn, cabbage, carrots, onion, cauliflower, and gourds of all colors are arranged on low planks and tagged with red, white, and blue ribbons. The still life depicts the pride and celebration of the farmers' labor. The saturation of warm tones gives a charmed cast to the image, and the reality presented by this and other color photographs by Lee engages us in a different way than the sense of nostalgic despair that a black-and-white images might; the use of color results in a truly sympathetic document of American history.

1. W. Ralph Eubanks, "Fields of Vision," in *Fields of Vision: The Photographs of Russell Lee,* ed. Nicholas Lemann (Washington DC: Library of Congress, 2008), xi.

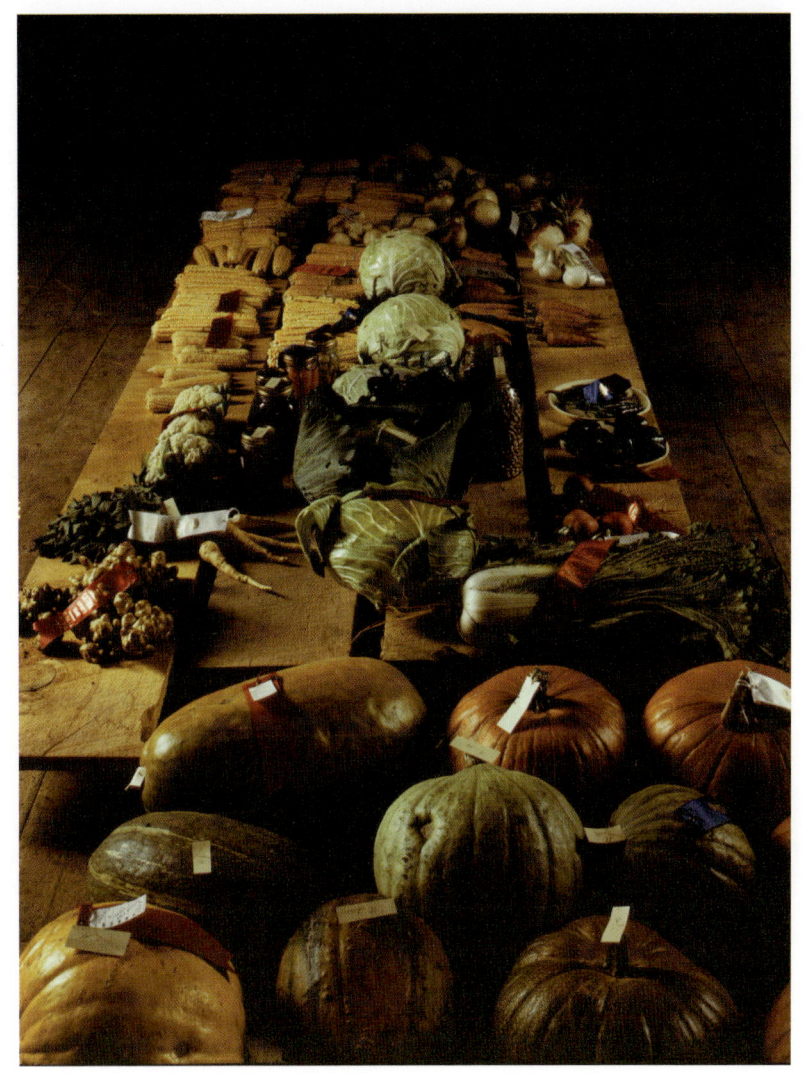

Russell Lee
Exhibit of crops and vegetables at the Pie Town, New Mexico, Fair, 1940
Digital print from original transparency, 19.5 x 25"

Thomas Ruff
by Gregory Ruppe

Most of the photos we come across today aren't really authentic anymore – they have the authenticity of a manipulated and prearranged reality.

—Thomas Ruff

Since the early 1980s, German-born artist Thomas Ruff has challenged perceptions of truth and fiction in the photographic image. He employs a systematic approach to creating pictures, combining techniques of appropriation, digital manipulation, and infrared imaging as a way of forcing tension between what we see and what we think we see.

For more than two decades, he has assigned no hierarchy to his pictorial discoveries, but approaches each new subject with the same clarity and objectivity as the previous one. Study under Bernd and Hilla Becher at the Kunstakademie Düsseldorf instilled in him this methodical approach. Like the Bechers, his photography is Apollonian, quasi-scientific, and recalls the style of early twentieth-century New German photographers such as August Sander. But Ruff distinguishes himself quickly from his mentors by using color, a move that radically challenges the presumed authenticity of the documentary-like black-and-white image.

Ruff's L.M.V.D.R. series, to which the *d.p.b.* photographs belong, is no exception to his rule of subtle subversion. Beginning in 1999, he combined straight photography and digital manipulation to capture the innovative spirit of Ludwig Mies van der Rohe's modernist masterpiece, the German Pavilion for the 1929 International Exhibition in Barcelona, Spain. Mies's building was dismantled following the closing of the exhibition and remained an archetype of modern architecture, known only in black-and-white photographic form for more than fifty years, until it was reconstructed in the mid-1980s. Ruff approached documentation of the monument by focusing on the architect's emphasis on "not the what, but the how."[1] In *d.p.b. 03, 04, 05* and *07*, Ruff serially altered a photograph of the Pavilion's interior curtains.

At first glance, the photographs are typologies in the truest sense. As a group, they appear to serially document curtains of different hues.

Although the images' composition highlights Mies's quadrangular elements and dynamic sensibility, Ruff's approach remains dead-pan and scientific. Each image acts like a microscopic slide, preserving a sample of the Pavilion's architectural unity. But knowing that Ruff digitally altered the colors of the curtains essentially creates a typology of deception. The reality of the serial variation is a manipulation of fact, or only true in the way that we perceive the photographic plane.

Most of us take photographic information for granted as a form of documentation or a kind of evidence. Based on what we see (or what we think we see), we habitually project what we think we know onto a subject in search of deeper meaning. But this can inhibit or even negate our understanding of a work of art. Ruff believes that "photography can only reproduce the surface of things;"[2] therefore nothing can be revealed about the photographic subject other than its formal state of representation.

Ruff applies Bernd Becher's assertion that an image produced distinctly resonates its means of production. That is why the art-photographer's willingness to experiment with new technologies and processes while retaining the medium's identity so successfully challenges and shifts the boundaries of photography.

Beyond experimentation, Ruff's photographs, more importantly, employ archetypes as subject matter to question the accepted iconic form of an image. As in his color manipulations of Mies's architectural icon, we are left to ponder the content or meaning of the images. Perhaps the adjustment of hue is the artist's interpretation of Mies's innovative spirit. Or perhaps Ruff is once again investigating the veracity of photography and toying with our tendency to believe what we see.

1. Zwirner & Wirth and David Zwirner, "Thomas Ruff, *l.m.v.d.r*," exhibition press release, September 2011, http://www.zwirnerandwirth.com/exhibitions/2001/092001Ruff/press.html
2. Viviane Rehberg, "Surface Tension: Viviane Rehberg on Thomas Ruff." *Tate Magazine*, no.5, (May/June 2002). http://www.tate.org.uk/magazine/issue5/ruff.htm

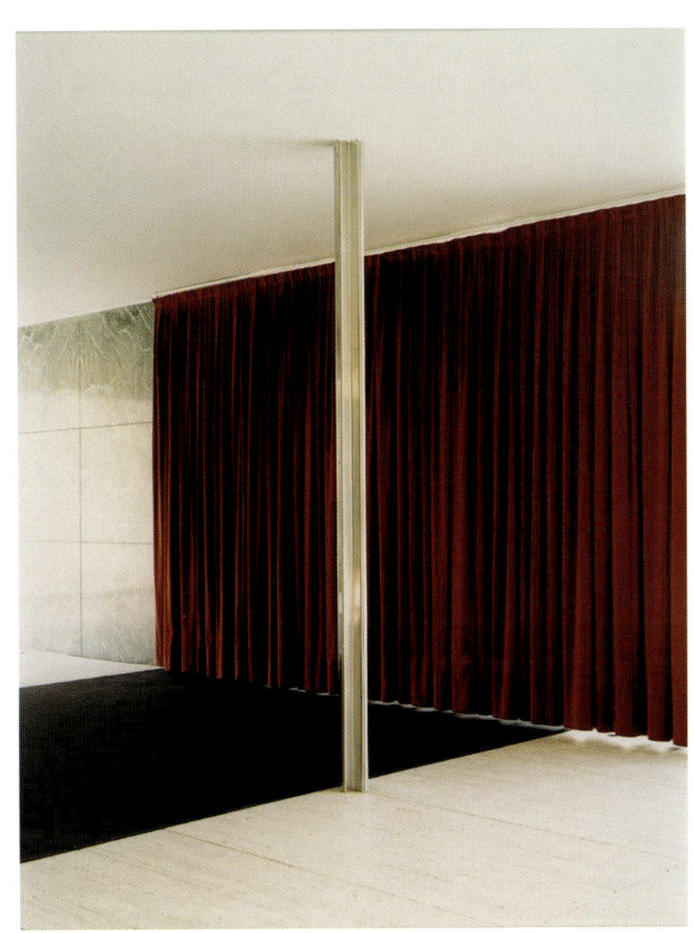
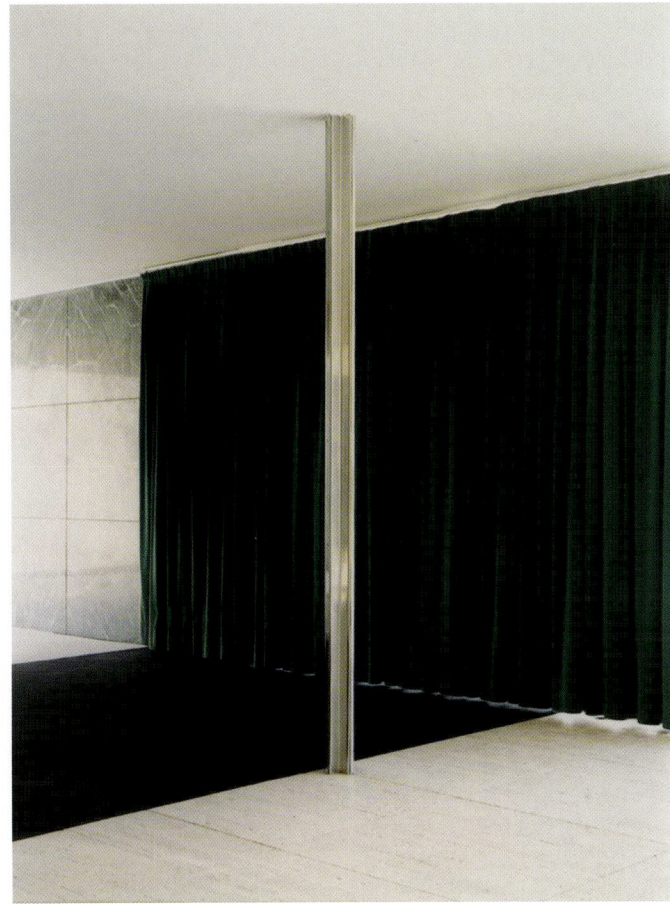

Thomas Ruff

d. p. b. 03, 1999
C-print, 11.5 x 8.5"

d. p. b. 04, 1999
C-print, 11.5 x 8.5"

Stephen Shore
by Melissa Barry

Finding beauty in the banal, Stephen Shore's deceptively simple photographs capture the ordinariness of rural and urban America and render it memorable. Traversing the country in the 1970s on numerous road trips, Shore produced his two best-known bodies of work: American Surfaces and Uncommon Places. The New York-based artist embarked on his first road trip in the summer of 1972, documenting the mundane moments he encountered, such as the lunch stops, waitresses, and attendants at full-service gas stations, as well as main streets, motels, and unmade beds. "I was just really amazed by all these things I was encountering," recalls Shore, "what my motel room looked like, and what the food looked like. Within a day or two, I realized I wanted to keep a kind of visual diary of the trip—to record every person I met, and every meal, and every bed."[1]

This genuine, nonjudgmental approach to his vernacular subject matter is perhaps indebted to his time spent in Andy Warhol's Factory, where between 1965 and 1969 Shore was invited to photograph and document parties and happenings. Self-taught and without a formal art education, Shore learned about photography from first-hand experience and what he gleaned from the Factory subculture, such as an interest in consumer culture and mass-produced techniques. In fact, American Surfaces, characterized by a casual snapshot quality, was taken with the easy-to-use, handheld 35mm Rollei camera (a precursor of the point-and-shoot). Not only were the tourist-like photographs developed as if in a Kodak lab—unthinkable for a fine-art photographer, the unframed snapshots were pasted directly on the gallery wall for exhibition. "I think for a lot of people who entered the room it was like colored wallpaper," Shore reflects.[2]

For Uncommon Places, which includes *La Brea Avenue and Beverly Boulevard, Los Angeles, 1975* (1975) and *Presidio, Texas, February 21, 1975* (1975) Shore traded in his Rollei camera for the larger format 8 x 10 camera, which allowed for immense clarity and increased depth of field. Far more structured and controlled than in American Surfaces, Shore exploited the capabilities of the larger camera to re-present the vast sprawl and subtleties of the landscape: "If I saw something interesting, I didn't have to make a picture *about* it. I could let it be somewhere in the picture, and have something else happen as well. So this changes the function of the picture—it's not like pointing at something and saying, 'Take a look at this.' It's saying, 'Take a look at this object I'm making.' It's asking you to savor not something in the world, but to savor the image itself."[3]

One of the pioneering figures of color photography in the early 1970s, Shore was included in the seminal 1975 photography show "New Topographics: Photographs of a Man-Altered Landscape." Significant for being the only color photography in the exhibition, Shore's photographs, which included *Presidio, Texas*, punctuated the exhibition with the scarlet neon lights on a movie theater, the tawny hotel bedspread, the ochre facade of a drive-in movie, and clear blue skies. As Peter Schjeldahl has commented on color photography, "Black and white can show what something is. Color adds how it is, imbued with the temperatures and humidities of experience."[4] Whether the dusty dirt roads of Texas or the avocado greens and mustard yellows of automobiles, the hues in Shore's photographs tell *how* these subjects and his experiences were in 1970s America.

1. Christy Lange, "Nothing Overlooked," in *Stephen Shore* (New York: Phaidon Press, 2007), 59.
2. Michael Fried, "Interview," in *Stephen Shore*, 9.
3. Lange, "*Stephen Shore*," 87, 92.
4. Peter Schjeldahl, "Alone with Baseball: Stephen Shore's Minor League," *Aperture*, no. 172 (Fall 2003): 18-23.

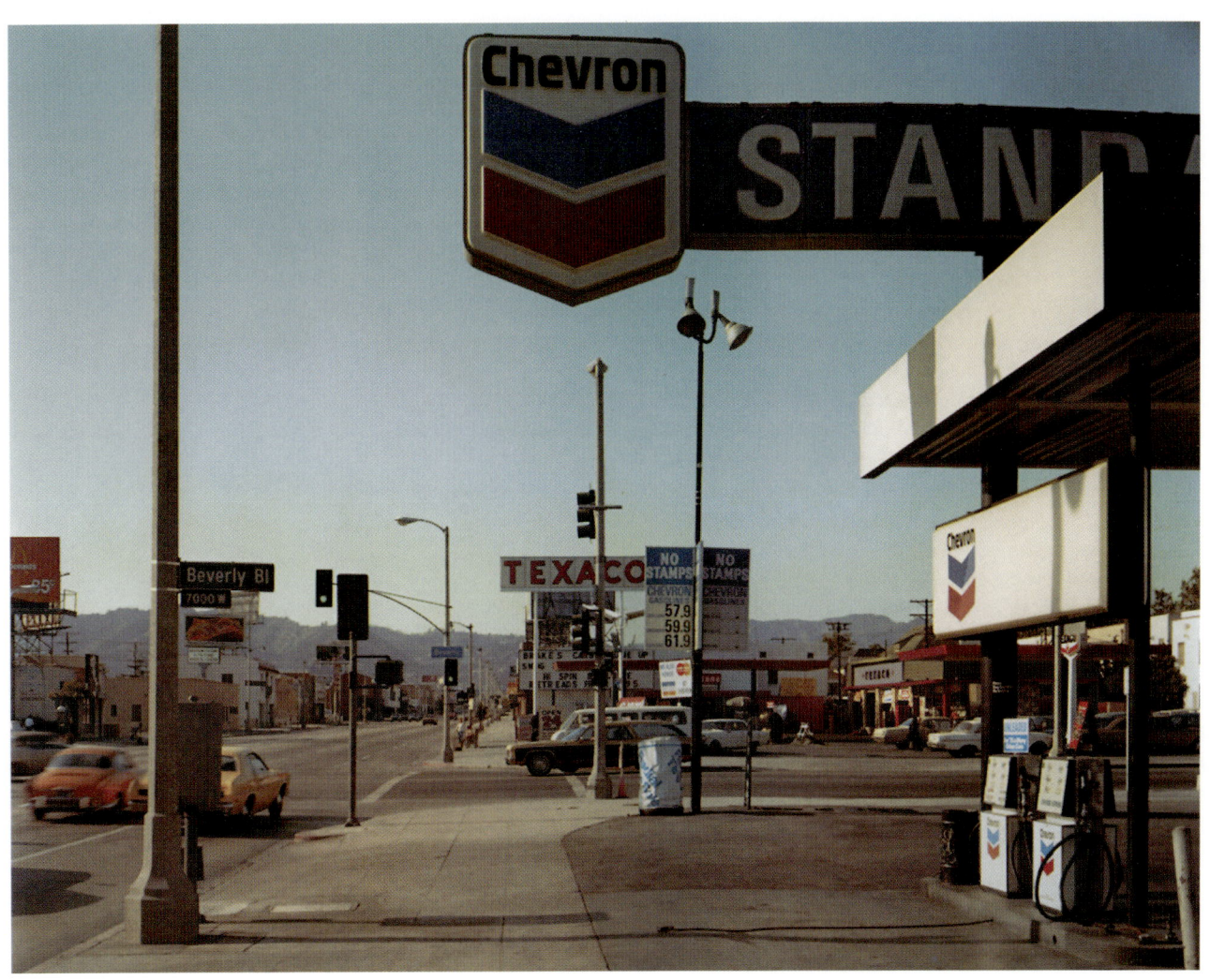

Stephen Shore

La Brea Avenue and Beverly Boulevard, Los Angeles, 1975, 1975

Vintage Chromogenic (or color coupler) print, 17 x 21.5"

Allison V. Smith
by Meg Smith

Allison V. Smith is a contemporary photographer whose work blurs the line between editorial and fine art. Smith's "passion for taking pictures" began at fifteen, when her parents enrolled her in a Young Photographers workshop at the Maine Photographic Workshop in Rockport, Maine—a place where her family still has a home and she frequents annually.[1] A native of Dallas, Smith went on to study journalism at Southern Methodist University and was able to marry her two interests by becoming a photojournalist. For nearly twenty years, Smith was on staff at such publications as the *Fort Worth Star Telegram* and the *Dallas Morning News*; her work has also been featured in the *New York Times*, *Esquire*, and *The New Yorker*. Needing a more creative outlet, however, she made an abrupt change to her career and became a freelance photographer in 2003.

Smith's photographic epiphany was realized following a road trip to Marfa, Texas, where she felt "liberated" after being able to shoot pictures for herself. Smith's images of the Marfa landscape have since developed into an extensive ongoing series that initiated a similar project on the Maine coast, of which *Bell. July 2011. Penobscot Bay, Maine, Nonesuch. August 2009. Rockport, Maine, and Saddle Island. August 2010. Penobscot Bay, Maine* are pristine examples.

Inspired by the beauty found in everyday locales, Smith uses her camera to record the commonplace in contemporary life, such as a bell buoy or flora. She describes her stylistic approach as being attracted to "simplicity," whether it is a tripartite composition consisting of sky, figure, and ground (land or sea), or single pops of color. Yet, she does not actively seek out her subject matter; rather, she describes her photographic process as being an outcome of "responding to wherever she is at the moment."

The archetypal thread through Smith's work is her intent to "present the world to viewers in a way they might not have seen before." The primary means by which she accomplishes her objective is with the use of a Hasselblad film camera. The square-format photographs produced by the Hasselblad result in an image frame that differs from customary visual perception, particularly landscape vision; thus, Smith effectively challenges her audience to take the time to look and reflect afresh. In doing so, she not only gives her audience the opportunity to sense the poetic susceptibility apparent in her serene yet simple treatment of composition and color, but also demonstrates her personal connection to objects and places in Maine.

[1] All quotes and paraphrases are based on an interview with the artist by the author, Dallas, February 9, 2012.

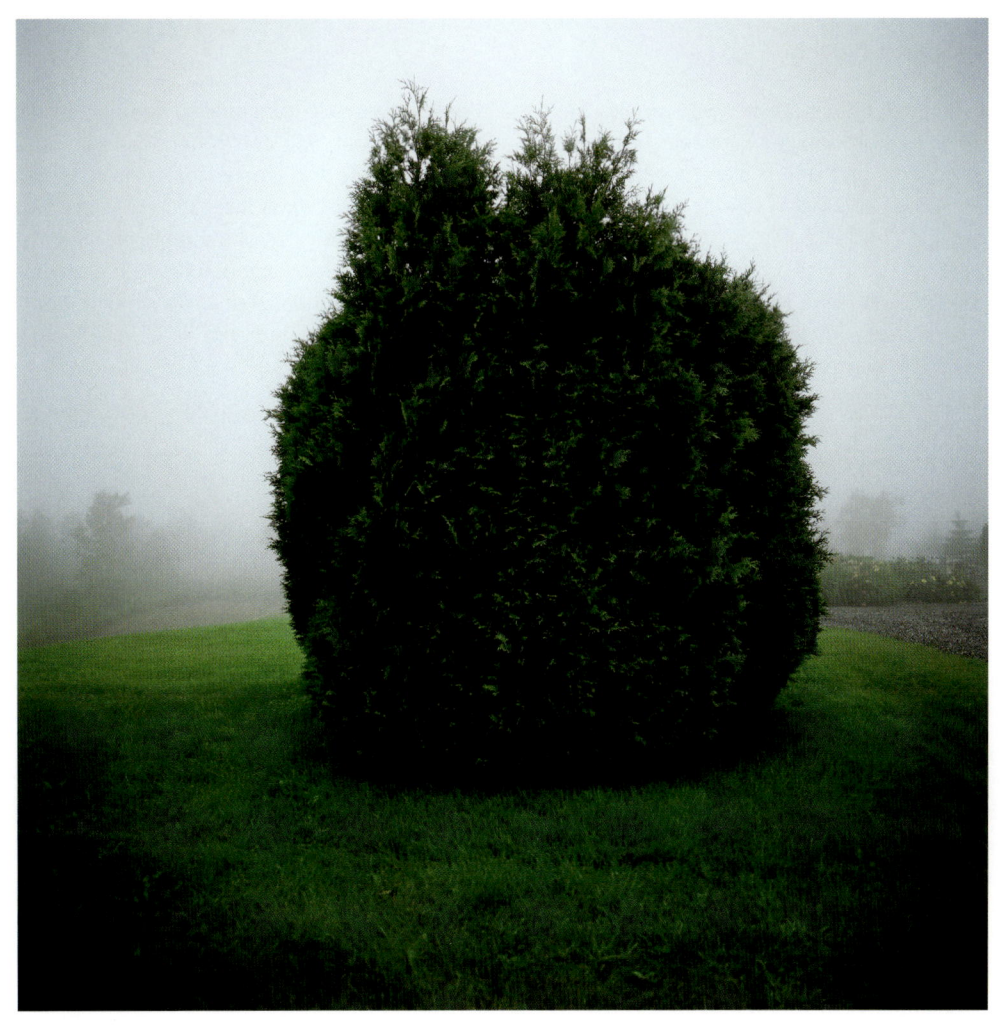

Allison V. Smith

Nonesuch. August 2009. Rockport, Maine, 2010
Chromogenic color photograph, edition 1/3, 40 x 40"

Ann Stautberg
by David Cavaliero and Devon Nowlin

As technology progresses, so does the artist's ability to employ an expanding color spectrum and to make images increasingly vibrant. Describing color as "vibrant" seems particularly fitting here because it characterizes something as having abounding energy or enthusiasm: in the case of Ann Stautberg's *7.11.07 PM, #11*, "vibrant" translates to being full of life. Distinguishing the things around us in color allows us to not only appreciate the subtleties in a work of art, but it is also integral to our evolution and survival as a species in our ability to gage the health and viability of life surrounding us. The association of color with life, and vice versa, is not one of coincidence but a marker of how we situate ourselves within the visible world.

It is a natural progression to associate the absence of color with mortality, and explains the late-nineteenth and early-twentieth-century popularity of photographic colorization. Before the advent of color photography, hand tinting or painting black-and-white photographic portraits made them appear more realistic and life-like. However, compared to either traditional painting or color photography, hand-colorized photographs often boast an uncanny or surreal appearance, intensified by the impulse of the artist to enhance or preserve an image by subjectively colorizing it—an effect Stautberg emphasizes through her use of newer painting technologies as opposed to the older methods of colorization with water-based paints and stains.

The relative opacity of the oil paint does not tint her photograph so much as coat it with a heavily pigmented glow, and strikes the hibiscus flower with a hyper-bold red that is unachievable through other or earlier techniques. Bringing a nineteenth-century inspiration into contemporary practice, Stautberg explores the historic relationship between the addition of color where it was previously absent and the augmented sense of vitality it instills.

True mortality, however, is not something that is often fully perceived in a still portrait. We can identify most life forms as being young, middle-aged, or older, but in general terms, the specifics of an entire life cycle, from birth to death, is incomprehensible in an image from a single moment. In her series of red hibiscus flowers, titled with the date and time its image was documented with her camera, Stautberg suspends the fleeting life cycle of the flower, which, unlike a human's, is observable on a nearly day-to-day basis. Her colorization process that follows acts to extend that moment of life and preserve the flower while simultaneously reinforcing its symbolism as a *memento mori*—an object that serves as a reminder of mortality.

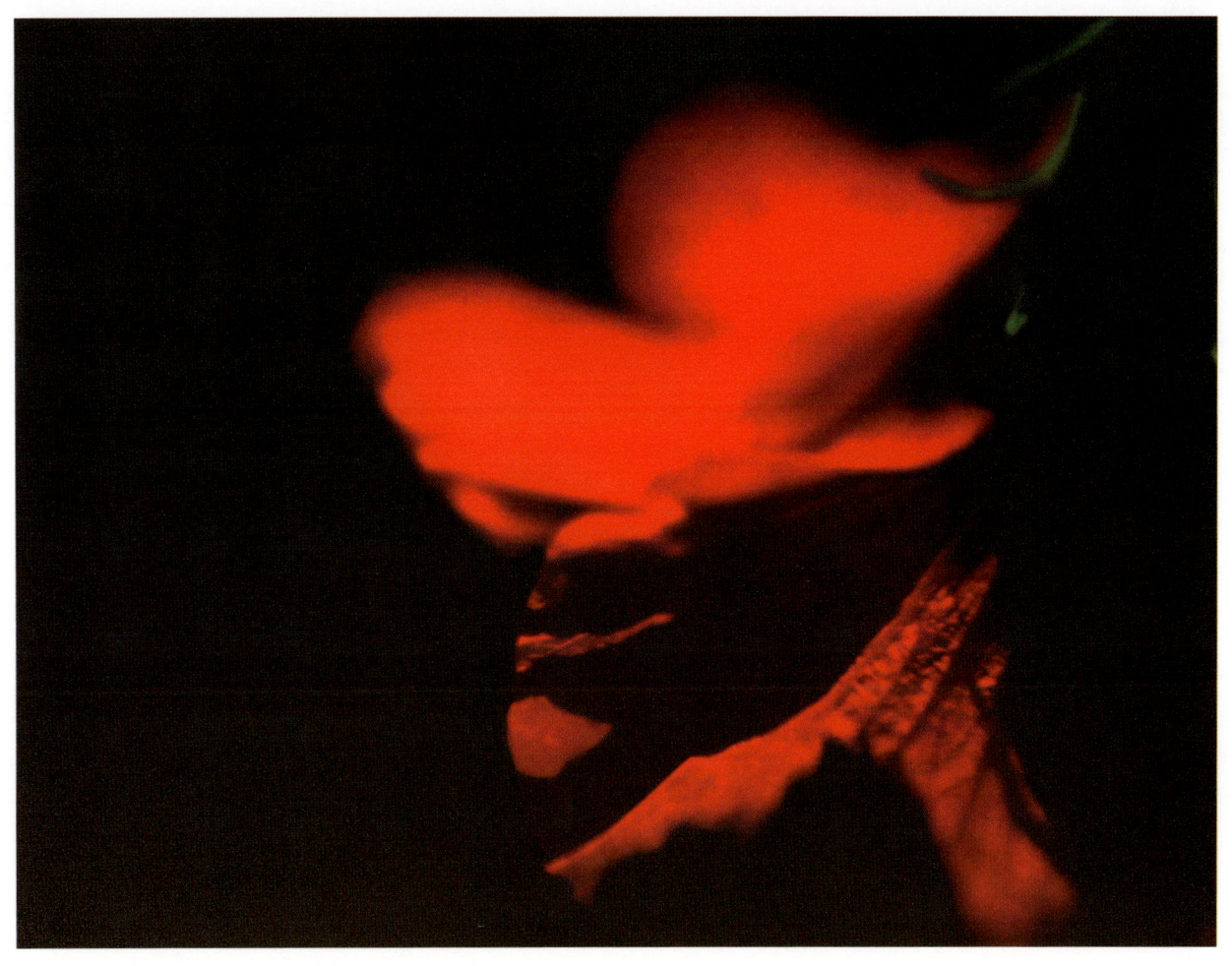

Ann Stautberg
7.11.07 PM, #11, 2007
Oil on black and white photograph, edition 1/9, 40 x 52"

Checklist

John Baldessari
Color Car Series: 1968 Volvo, Dirty and Polished, 1976/2011
Two archival inkjet prints, 15.75 x 19.75"; 16.25 x 20.25"

Courtesy of the artist and Margo Leavin Gallery, Los Angeles, CA

Sarah Charlesworth
Relative Values, Maximum Hues, 2006
Fuji Crystal archive print, 41 x 31"

Small Oval, 2006
Fuji Crystal archive print, 41 x 31"

Both Courtesy of the artist and Margo Leavin Gallery, Los Angeles, CA

William Eggleston
Greenwood, Mississippi, 1973
Vintage dye transfer print mounted to board, 12.5 x 19"

Collection of Catherine and Will Rose, Dallas, TX

Russell Lee
Exhibit of crops and vegetables at the Pie Town, New Mexico Fair, 1940
Digital print from original transparency, 25 x 19.5"

Jim Norris, homesteader, cutting a head of cabbage, Pie Town, New Mexico, 1940
Digital print from original transparency, 29 x 19.5"

Both Courtesy of the Library of Congress (exhibition copies)

Thomas Ruff
d. p. b. 03, 1999
C-print, 11.5 x 8.5"

d. p. b. 04, 1999
C-print, 11.5 x 8.5"

d. p. b. 05, 1999
C-print, 11.5 x 8.5"

d. p. b. 07, 1999
C-print, 11.5 x 8.5"

All Courtesy of The Rachofsky Collection, Dallas, TX

Stephen Shore
La Brea Avenue and Beverly Boulevard, Los Angeles, 1975, 1975
Vintage Chromogenic (or color coupler) print, 17 x 21.5"

Presidio, Texas, February 21, 1975, 1975
Vintage Chromogenic (or color coupler) print, 17 x 21.5"

Both Collection of Michael Auping, Fort Worth, TX

Allison V. Smith
Saddle Island. August 2010. Penobscot Bay. Maine, 2011
Chromogenic color photograph, edition 1/3, 40 x 40"

Nonesuch. August 2009. Rockport, Maine, 2010
Chromogenic color photograph, edition 1/3, 40 x 40"

Bell. July 2011. Penobscot Bay. Maine, 2011
Chromogenic color photograph, edition 1/3, 40 x 40"

All Courtesy of the artist and Barry Whistler Gallery, Dallas, TX

Ann Stautberg
7.11.07 PM, #11, 2007
Oil on black and white photograph, edition 1/9, 40 x 52"

Courtesy of the artist and Barry Whistler Gallery, Dallas, TX